A BRIEF RELIEF FROM HUNGER

SPENSER SMITH

Guelph, Ontari

T0035458

Edited by Shane Neilson
Cover and book design by Jeremy Luke Hill
Cover image by Syd Danger
Set in Linux Libertine
Printed on Mohawk Via Felt
Printed and bound by Arkay Design & Print

LIBRARY AND ARCHIVES CANADA CATALOGUING IN PUBLICATION

Title: A brief relief from hunger / Spenser Smith.
Names: Smith, Spenser, author.
Description: Poems.
Identifiers: Canadiana (print) 20230441610 | Canadiana (ebook) 20230441629 |
    ISBN 9781774220986 (softcover) | ISBN 9781774220993 (PDF) |
    ISBN 9781774221006 (EPUB)
Subjects: LCGFT: Poetry.
Classification: LCC PS8637.M5698 B75 2023 | DDC C811/.6—dc23

Gordon Hill Press gratefully acknowledges the support of the Canada Council for the Arts, the Ontario Arts Council, and the Ontario Book Publishing Tax Credit.

Gordon Hill Press respectfully acknowledges the ancestral homelands of the Attawandaron, Anishinaabe, Haudenosaunee, and Métis Peoples, and recognizes that we are situated on Treaty 3 territory, the traditional territory of Mississaugas of the Credit First Nation.

Gordon Hill Press also recognizes and supports the diverse persons who make up its community, regardless of race, age, culture, ability, ethnicity, nationality, gender identity and expression, sexual orientation, marital status, religious affiliation, and socioeconomic status.

Gordon Hill Press
130 Dublin Street North
Guelph, Ontario, Canada
N1H 4N4
www.gordonhillpress.com

Table of Contents

I

II

III

For Sam, Alan, David, and Derek.

I

Builder of sons

A kid, I'd watch *Cops* with you. Men
cruised murky streets, the safety inside

their Crown Vic not unlike our living
room. Formulaic plot: vehicle search,

drugs hidden under seats with fallen
French fries. Dad, when you found

needles in my pocket, did it feel
like a familiar scene? You tried

to teach me the difference between
rare and medium rare, the scam

of extended warranties, how survival
is like a hammered nail—it absorbs

blow after blow and makes a home
out of pressure. I was too scared

in Kindergarten to raise my hand
for the washroom so I wet myself.

I panicked when you took Turner
to the arcade without me, my chest

heaving like the rock dove I found
in Snowball's jaws. You are a nail.

You build sons who think, "Let me be
half the man my dad is." Half of you:

a hundred-car freight train ripping
through Regina at rush hour, a field

aflame with wildflowers and crickets.
I can't connect wood from blueprints

sketched in my head, our deck a reality
you dreamed last night. I can't repair

drywall but know if I asked, you'd
show. I survived seven-day binges,

overdoses, and scoops of peanut butter
for dinner because I picked up just enough

of your lessons. Not the practical tips
and tricks (I'm thirty and can't change

a tire), but the care. You, a teenager
who lost his father in a fire. I survived

because you remained
a sturdy structure.

Scratcher of backs

Twelve hours of corralling men
at the office. At home, you asked

for little: some space to smoke
your brand, some time to play

Solitaire.

*

Mom, when did you notice
who I'd become? Four sons

and two daughters, each child
a fledgling nation with breaking

news.

*

I stole your money, swiped
rest from your swollen joints.

You still did my laundry.
On the table, your labour

sorted and stacked.

*

Childhood nightmares led me
to your bed. Asleep, you'd pull

my body into your warmth.
All these years, the safety

I craved.

*

You and Dad drove to Saskatoon
each Sunday to visit me in treatment.

I bet the drive from Regina contained
not words, but sizzles in the Coke can

ashtray.

*

You have always been a sucker
for strays, your house a haven

for unnamed felines. Can a body hold
that much love, that much ache,

without wilting?

*

A tuck in, 1996. You scratch
my back and whisper secrets:

the child before me was miscarried.
But you, my sweet one, you are

alive.

*

Detox in Regina, Moose Jaw, Regina again.
Treatment in Trois-Rivières then Nanaimo.

I've seen such beautiful cuts
of this country, beautiful cuts

of you.

Let's go to The Lake

The Lake is a body of water I rarely enter while at The Lake.

The Lake is a neatly placed poster in an otherwise messy bedroom. I am a dirty sock. My brothers are dirty socks. My family, a mound of dirty socks.

The Lake is a lifestyle. Before arriving at The Lake, please purchase a "How Merlot Can You Go?" t-shirt from the general store.

The Lake is a Dodge Ram commercial but instead of a gruff voice questioning my manhood, tank-topped teenagers with bushy chests.

The Lake is a science experiment. Before arriving at The Lake, please document your chest hairs.

A dirty sock pops a pimple in The Lake.

The Lake is a twenty-minute drive from the city we live in but pretend doesn't exist. This is the wilderness, goddamn it!

The Lake is a bank and recyclables are the currency I withdraw. How else, after a twenty-minute drive back to the city, could I afford to get high?

The Lake holds northern pike, walleye, and dill pickle chip dust I wash from my fingers.

A dirty sock splashes another dirty sock in the face.

The Lake blooms with algae and a nearby crow calls it karma.

Hundreds of Men: A case study

Abstract: Even before the first known use of a hammer in 3,300,000 BCE, men have defined themselves by their ability to strike blunt objects against other blunt objects to complete complex tasks (e.g., shaping stones with stones, prehistoric mating rituals). In turn, men have traditionally performed jobs that value pride of force (e.g., carpentry, judicial execution). However, in a changing global job market in which men are more likely to slam a computer in frustration than slam a nail on a jobsite, the definition of what it means to be part of the collective called "men" is changing. This case study will analyze the manhood of its author against the manhood of men with roofing jobs to define "men" in the modern age and conclusively show that "men" is both a single word and a thousand cultures.

Keywords: Men, identity, man up, overtime, stubbed fingers, flexing.

Background and methods

In 1995, my dad started Prime Roofing Inc. I was four. Since then, I've observed hundreds of men he has employed, first as "the boss's son" and briefly as an employee in 2008.

This study will rely on interviews and observations from memory in both roofing and non-roofing environments.

Conflict of interest declaration

1. I am a man without an interest in hammers.

List of Prime Roofing Inc. roofing installers and labourers (1995 – 2004)

Cat-like men, cat-calling men, humble men, men who stumble on land but float on ladders, bruised men, bluesmen, men who hold their bladders, men with one set of clothes, small-nosed men, nine-toed men, men who say "women" with toothless gums, resurrected men, rejected men, men with dandelions for hearts, rational men, track-marked men, joking men, spokesmen, men with naked women tattoos, "that's true" men, wise men, wide-chested men, unprotected men, abused men, short-fused men, men who carry three bundles of shingles on one shoulder, older men, nameless men, wordless men, happy men, hopeful men, men with nails for teeth, mouthy men, Kokanee men, men with a light in exchange for a story, sorry men, men who smell like rain, paint-stained men, cash-only men, brave men, messy men, men on the mend.

Field notes #1 (June 26th, 1998, Age: 6)

Wordless Man sits shotgun in Dad's truck. I'm crammed between Kokanee Man and Wise Man in the back. My t-shirt absorbs their sweat, an omen.

Dad drives to the dump, Regina's only mountain, to dispose of a piano. The men are tired from working under the sun on a black roof. They reek of asphalt and sorrow.

> "Are you gunna be a roofer when you grow up?" Kokanee Man asks me.

> Dad's eyes appear in the rear-view mirror.

> "Course you are. Just like your old man," Kokanee Man answers.

> "Kid," Wise Man says, "you don't want to slave over a roof, back crouched, knees giving out."

> "And why fucking not?" Kokanee Man says.

> Wordless Man sits in the front seat, wordless.

Field notes #2 (November 23rd, 2002, Age: 11)

Want to see the website I built?

> *Hold the nail with your thumb and first finger.*

Want to see the website

> *Hold the handle closer to the head for superior control.*

Want to see

> *Make a small notch to hold the nail upright.*

Want

> *Let the flick of your wrist drive the nail.*

Field notes #3 (July 2nd, 2003, Age: 11)

On a nine-pitch roof
five men become cats
scruffy strays
slinking between
hips and valleys
paws prance
to the blare
of AC/DC
the machine
gun spray
of nails

Interview #1 (September 21st, 2004, Age: 12)

The following interview was conducted for a grade eight "Career Day" project.

Name: Spokesman
Age: 33
Roofing experience: 11 years

Q: What's it like being a roofer?

A: My life is the hammer my life is the rattle
tall ladders spat gravel the bang bang bang
the hang before the lift socks full of sift tasting
asphalt and piss the steel sunrise songs
five nails right four nails wrong
my life is the crackle my life is tarspackle
burnt skin black apples the sun eating
lips curled toes bruised hips clak clak
bone chips

List of Prime Roofing Inc. roofing installers and labourers (2004 – 2012)

Mendacious men, men with pens, men without friends, deep-end men, "extra cheese, no veggies" men, kale men, keen men, men who stir puddles into beer, craving men, unshaven men, men who can't fend, tender men, men who rate women from 1 to 10, gregarious men, precarious men, men with cauliflower ears, men who breathe sunflower seeds, first-rate men, second chance men, men who take meds, men who refuse meds, NFL men, VLT men, menstruating men, men who love CNN, cement men, men with dads, men without dads, men who are dads now and again, modest men, mean men, mild men, childish men, men with shingles for skin, cool-skinned men, scarred men, men with joints with your name on them, high men, mentoring men, paycheck to paycheck men, men who show up time and again, men who make amends.

Field notes #4 (December 19th, 2006, Age: 15)

Dad and High Man huddle in the doorway of our home.

"This is the last time," High Man says. "I promise."

His Prime Roofing hoodie is dotted with circular burns. His eyes, two circular burns.

Dad smacks a bill into High Man's hand.

"This is the last time," Dad says. "I promise."

Questions for further research (June 29th – August 27th, 2008, Age: 16)

During the summer before grade twelve, I worked as a roofing labourer and posed a series of questions to co-workers on my crew. The following questions were left unanswered.

How long did the guy before last?
Does tetanus sting?
Is that tar or a shadow?
A thrush or a sparrow?
Are you drunk?
Is "drunk" a synonym for "brave"?
Can I have a sip?
Is that a scare-owl or an owl-owl?
What's thirty feet to my spine?
Appropriate response: silence, "shit," or "ow ow ow"?
Muscle cramps—a synonym for thirst?
Stealing hose water—a crime?
How long does midnight oil take to burn?
Is payday worth it?
At the end of the day, who pays more?
Payback—a bitch or a noun?

Conclusion

Men
/men/

The controlled movements and expert momentary judgements of the documented Prime Roofing Inc. employees are comparable to the acumen of experienced airmen. Though, in the field of construction, the mentality necessary to withstand such regiments is often unlamented. It is worth mentioning that, even without childhood mentors, these men manage meaningful employment and momentous personal achievements. While the craft of roofing is typically looked at as menial, it offers attractive, incremental payment structures, tremendous physical benefits, and amenable working environments. As the study's featured specimen, I lacked the rudimentary skills needed to succeed in roofing (e.g., an interest in hammers, endurance of physical torment). It could be argued that a glance at my abdomen would be enough to come to this conclusion. While similar studies have shown that men who lack these rudimentary skills earn only enough to survive on a menu of instant ramen, I hope to avoid this phenomenon.

Welcome to Vancouver

Cigarette smoke pours
through my range hood.
In another world, I pound

my apartment neighbour's
face, order him to stop
feeding me his lung

cancer. In this world,
I cough before inhaling
a five-dollar doughnut.

A short walk away
at Main and Hastings,
fellow humans exist

without range hoods.
Once, I shot coke
in my bedroom

while Grandma cooked
cabbage rolls in the kitchen.
After my rush faded,

we ate like equals.

II

Sweet soil

*Plenty of forest land, go out there, dig a hole, sit in it and do a
double dose of fentanyl and a Bobcat will come along and fill
in the hole and we can start all over again.*
– Facebook comment

3.

I dig a hole in the forest with Grandma's garden spade. Sitting in
the open wound, I wait for a Bobcat to spill sweet soil over my
blistered hands, over my swollen body. Chickadees chirp, oaks
creak, but no machine arrives. Instead, a bobcat. Golden eyes,
ears tipped with black trophies, the cat paws soil into the hole.
Tongue stretched, I catch the falling earth and taste insects who
will soon nibble my skin.

2.

Grandma's garden: coneflower, ninebark, cranesbill. Their roots
quiver from my footsteps. The air, tickling my neck with ladybug
legs, smells purple. In the green compost bin lie half-chewed
perogies. I can't stomach food or shame, but my leftovers will
breed life. Beside the pipe-smoking gnome, a spade.

1.

In the kitchen, we sit in the silence of my scrolling. I know you're
high, Grandma says without words, but you must eat. I accept
her offer of cheddar perogies. The recipe has survived diphtheria
and droughts. Who am I to say no?

The cost of junk

*It would be cheaper to clean up the dead junkies than saving their lives
on a weekly, even daily basis...*
– Facebook comment

It would be cheaper to let dead junkies rot. Crow food. A free
        "This Is Your Brain on Drugs" commercial.

It would be cheaper to dissect dead junkies in biology class. Eliminate
        the need to purchase crayfish, piglets, sheep eyes.

It would be cheaper to request payment for dead junkies. Charge
        families for breeding burdens.

Is it possible to love junkies? Bruises, inflamed livers, knees
        first scraped on playgrounds.

It will take a new vocabulary to love junkies. One without the word
        "junkie."

Love takes work. Step one: do not kill the spider dangling
        from the shower curtain. Instead, cradle its body with tissue.

Dog backwards is god

*lock em up and euthanize them if they refuse treatment, they
dont have any more dignity than a stray dog so why treat
them any different than the dog pound treats the stray.*

– Facebook comment

You lie
        at my feet
in a needle-laced
        alley. I kneel
and stroke the fur
        on your starved
throat, my hands
        a tease of meat
and bone. Hunger
        is a reminder
of the cost to live—
        bite or die.
I ask for your name
        and you expose
a matted belly
        filled with sidewalk
water and hope.
        I'm hungry.
For warmth.
        Fried chicken.
A gram of coke
        or two or three.
Let's be friends,
        dog. But first,
stop wagging
        your tail.
My touch
        is no substitute
for protein.

Policy proposal

They should be lined up and needles thrown at them like darts.
– Facebook comment

Bodies lined up
like old bottles.
The best bullseye
is a body
clothed in nothing
but bruises
and starlight.
The best bullseye
is my body,
braced for contact,
forever curled
like a shrimp.
Needles splay
my chest.
Ten points
for a nipple,
says the sheriff,
twenty
for an eye.

Small deaths

Eventually the problem should fix itself, just sayin...
– Facebook comment

Death is an ant under your shoe,
the unwatered spider plant,
a grain of fentanyl
thinner than a needle
of Douglas fir.

*

I search the rainforest
for names of the dead.
Unlike the newspaper,
there are no statistics here,
only red alder, sword fern.

*

Vancouver grew so sick
of rain it built a coffee shop
on every corner.

How many downpours
until we upend earth
for solutions?

How many deaths?

*

I find an obituary
etched into the skin
of an arbutus.
Alan enjoyed great food,
especially prosciutto.

Overhead, a barred owl
flies.

How many men

how many men before

how many

how many men before we

how many men

women and men

men men men

many women

many many men

how many

how many men

how many men and when

before we

before you

dead men before you

how many

how many men

how and when

how and when

We met on 5th

January

You twist a latex-free tourniquet around my bicep. Blood pools. Departure restricted. I notice your birth year tattooed on your forearm and calculate the alarming math. Twenty-feet behind this door, my grandma crafts cabbage rolls with depression-era precision. Her kitchen is a shrine of bucket tupperware and dandelion bouquets. Nothing wasted. A prick, pull, and you send my **body** home.

Warmth. Not unlike 1999, cuddled up, watching re-runs of *The Simpsons* after a fried hot dog feast.

March

I imagine the sweet things your **family** might say about you, the usual yearbook evidence: the bowl cut you wore with pride, the sport you loved and never imagined giving up. I've mapped what's left of the veins in your arms, not out of anything like love but duty.

July

Surround yourself with only **addicts** (a necessary survival act) and your name will gradually dissolve.

body

body ache [chills in a hot shower] the body's narcotic cravings, inject the body [lifting a spoon] body temperature swing, disintegrating body [ears ringing] his body, another man's body [911 dispatcher] body stretched out, she shook the body ["get up" and "come on"] police found ██████'s body, the provincial health body: [undated photo] turn the body over

family

CBC News has spoken to family and friends of ██████████, a powerlifter who loved fishing and family.

██████████████████ openly discusses the addiction that has strained her family for years, hoping others can talk about family, instead of hiding out of shame.

"We were arguing all the time—about my family, about my parenting, my job, my family, my freedom."

"I was afraid for my family, the very fabric of family, afraid I'd lose my job, afraid of what other people would say."

Her family, a large family, first tried to put her in a treatment program.

It devastated her father, ██████████████, who described ████ ████ to CBC News as the "anchor" of her family.

People who were there told the family ██████████ took "one hoot" of the opioid. Paramedics weren't called for two hours, her family said. Friends told family she was battling a fentanyl addiction her family thought she had nearly beaten.

██████████ reached out to friends and family members, who wrote loving memories of the woman they knew as kind, generous, sweet and hard-working.

"For us as a family, we were living in absolute hell and couldn't understand it," said ██████████.

"Family was the most important thing."

addicts

a common problem
facing

addicts:
addicts

have no shortage
of negative

emotions
addicts

just
skirt

consequences
addicts

relapse
addicts

are a
common

problem
solution:

get
addicts

lock(ed) up
addicts

push
addicts

(recovering
addicts)

into
long

sentences

August

You sift ashtray sand outside Galaxy Cinemas, fingers deep, stoking smoke. Pores blessed, momentarily, by liquid aerosol, a formaldehydic feat of incomplete combustion. Bless you. Bless the human being who could have left enough tobacco in one of these butts but didn't. Your hands are the hands of a human being. The dignity in being, scorched like nicotine.

Fruit fly trap

B.C. is a bowl of apple cider
vinegar and dish detergent, a sweet
trap designed to drown. I escape

the swat of your hand, my body
nearly another smear on the wall.
Pour Drano

down the pipes. Scald our wings
into nothingness. Did you know
the lifespan of a fruit fly

is 30 to 50 days? So short,
getting shorter
by the month.

Dear Sam

You roamed Vancouver like a myth.

Heroin in our drug-free home.

Bliss, a barred owl gorging a squirrel
after a long hunt, before blackness.

Am I close?

Sam, I am sorry.

Comments:

It's called a Death Trip for a reason. We all have choices to make
while we are Alive.

Don't do drugs. It's not an illness it's a choice you made when it
was presented. I AM ALIVE!

Crime rate is dropping like junkies. Love it.

https://en.wikipedia.org/wiki/Culling

you pay your money, you take your chances.... the cull continues

Dear Mac Miller

I carry your voice in my pocket and summon it like a dose of naloxone. Sometimes I need reviving. Sometimes I listen to you, and only you.

You are the rich, famous version of me and my childhood friends. Sweet when you want to be. Full of depression, big dreams, and oxy.

Right now, someone listens to your voice without knowing you're a ghost. Fentanyl killed you one day before my brother's

wedding in Saskatchewan. Post-ceremony, my friend Alan texted to say Sam died: "See we only get so many chances."

Comments:

Does frequent naloxone use minimize its effectiveness? Let's hope the harm reduction strategy which is saving lives doesn't give addicts a superman complex.

hmm... that's where my money goes... to save useless idiots who voluntarily try to kill themselves... nice nice

Wouldn't it be awesome if diabetics got free needle and insulin kits to take home?

ban the kits let mother natural take its course

Our government = enablers

#Eastvan, sad place.

darwin's theory

omg

Dear Alan

Remember your 25th birthday? Desperate for a tattoo, though you didn't have a design in mind, just needed ink ASAP. After settling for a scummy studio in Harewood, you chose two words to grace your bicep: "Made It." A vape-smoking artist needled your decision permanent.

I said it was a nice tattoo, even though it was stupid. I can't remember what we did afterward. Probably devoured McDoubles, skated the parking lot beside my sober home. And after that, you landed in prison. Then Colony Farm. Then you overdosed on fentanyl. You are dead.

You are bodiless, Alan, posing for my camera at Bonnell Creek, throwing up peace signs in ladybug garden gloves. Wearing a broken skateboard as a hat, nudging me to call Value Village and get honest about my job interview lies. Sharing your 24th birthday with the 5th of Kirsten's daughter, letting her and the other kindergarteners climb your body in the hot tub. (Your dead body.) You both blowing out candles on a Disney princess cake. Alan, you made it.

Comments have been turned off for this post.

Prayer for the nameless

amenamenamenamenamenamenamenamenamenamenamenamena
menamenamenamenamenamenamenamenamenamenamenamenam
enamenamenamenamenamenamenamenamenamenamenamenamen
amnamenamenamenamenamenamenamenamenamenamenamename
namenamenamenamenamenamenamenamenamenamenamenamena
menamenamenamenamenamenamenamenamenamenamenamename
namenamenamenamenamenamenamenamenamenamenamenamena
menamenamenamenamenamenamenamenamenamenamenamenam
enamenamenamenamenamenamenamenamenamenamenamenamen

III

Treatment: Three Yelp reviews

Calder Centre (Youth program)
Saskatoon, Saskatchewan

★ ★ ★ ☆ ☆

Not allowed to smoke but otherwise the place was chill. Free food, free Nicorette, and nightly smudging. Detoxed with the help of orange juice and *Coach Carter*. Would have given 5/5 if not for A.A. meetings. When I refused to stand and recite "The Lord's Prayer," old men (who smelled of sugary Folgers and dust) told me I would die drunk.

Narconon
Trois-Rivières, Quebec

★ ☆ ☆ ☆ ☆

Knew something was up when staff handed me a stack of L. Ron Hubbard books. For fifty days, I drank olive oil and bird seed before sweating six straight hours in a sauna. Also yelled at ashtrays. When I emailed my parents to get me out, they didn't believe me (pawned too much of their stuff to hold any trust = genius business plan by Narconon). Gave up on sobriety and smoked smuggled weed out of a can with a Croatian giant named Ivan. Unless you're into Scientology, AVOID!

Edgewood
Nanaimo, British Columbia

★ ★ ★ ★ ☆

Edgewood's group therapy = good shit. Found some hope by sharing my story with others who shared similar. Counsellors had degrees and were (to my knowledge) legit. Low-key developed an eating disorder, though. Traded drugs for ketchup chips and Coffee Crisps and thirds of everything.

(Shout out to Edgewood's kitchen staff—you make the best beef stroganoff.)

1998 is a ministicks tournament played in a mantis green kitchen

Turned wrists parry plastic.
Your brother, a Potvin wannabe,
guards the heat vent net.

His mean hip check
propels your face
towards a mouthful
of porcelain tile.

You taste the familiar crumbs
of your mother's unique cuisine.

Kimchi.
Shake 'n Bake.
Coffee-rubbed steak.

Gustation is nostalgic,
organic compounds forging
delectable dichotomies.

Sweet or bitter.
Sour or salty.
Leave or stay.

2014: Across the country
you prepare avocados
in a $700, clean, 1 bdrm.
The rhythmic chop
against your bamboo
cutting board
slices the unsavory
silence, the lack
of intimacy
between you
and marble
linoleum.

Dream journal and interpretation from a sober, hungry addict

1.

The golden arches fall. A barred owl lays eggs inside the "o" in "McDonalds."

I ate Big Macs so I could quit drugs. I used drugs because I could not stomach shame.

2.

My Facebook feed, free of fast-food ads, teaches me to make Grandma's cabbage rolls.

A kid, I watched Grandma shake salt on everything.

A kid, I stripped the rolls of their cabbage and ate only the rice, beef, and pork.

3.

Restaurant debit machines ask, "How are you?" before asking for a tip.

I tip extra when the too-short legs of my table are left napkinless and free to wobble.

I tip extra when the waiter acknowledges I am dining alone.

I tip extra when my fortune cookie predicts the past.

4.

My continued sobriety rests on a skill testing question: "Is Pepsi okay?"

Coke versus Pepsi.
Heroin versus coke.

5.

On a diner table sits a plate of fries, an Everything Breakfast, and a Triple King Burger. I place the food on a giant spoon, which I melt with a giant lighter.

Fries – An upgrade from a diet of aluminum foil and smoke.

Everything Breakfast – Because I consumed breakfast with the speed and teeth of a garburator, my nickname in treatment was "Garby."

Triple King Burger –
2018: Alan and Sam die from fentanyl.
2014: Sober, we stroll Commercial Street. Don't spend a cent. Don't eat a thing.

6.

I shed my belly and develop cheese grater abs. Not to flex at the beach or in the bedroom. No, just to grate cheese.

If my stomach is a tool, my body is an overflowing toolshed.

7.

I become a barred owl

and swallow one hundred squirrels.

Comment section

comment
comment
comment
comment
comment
comment
comment
comment
comment
comment
comment
comment
comment
comment
comment
comment
comment
comment
comment
comment
comment
comment
comment
comment
comment
comment
comment
comment
comment
comment
comment
comment
comment
comment
comment
comment
comment
comment

Birdwatching

1. Short-eared owl

Only the flesh of a vole
will satisfy the growl

        of a short-eared owl.

Along the Fraser River delta
lies a cache

        of contaminants:

lead shells,
plastic bags,

        homeowners.

2. American robin

Waits for worms
to rise from mud

        like a game

of whack-a-mole.
A trillion sunrises,

        the same trill

and dance.

3. Anna's hummingbird

Fights weapon warfare—
beaks like swords,

        nectar
        the sweetest

dope.

4. Northern pygmy-owl

An owl
the heft

        of a tennis ball

gobbles prey
thrice its size:

        northern flicker,

northern bobwhite,
small pets

        in the northern

hemisphere.
Northern pygmy-owl,

        supposed king

of the north,
breakfast

        for the barred owl.

5. Barred owl

I found god
not in Narcotics

      Anonymous,

but a park
near Pizza Hut.

      Dear barred owl,

stiff on the gravel,
did you eat

      a poisoned rat?

Was it worth it,
your brief relief

      from hunger?

Dear David

I creeped your Facebook—it's how I check for vital signs, the temperature of bodies two provinces away. A stream of comments signaled cold skin. *RIP. WTF. The good die young.* I clicked your obituary, and my laptop slideshowed your life. Little David in a Toy Story shirt. Drug dealer David with a gold chain. *His gift to gab made every moment with him an adventure.* Yes, you were a talker. Your go-to salutation, "guy man bro," was Regina famous. Once, you brainstormed my obituary out loud, said I was *a fake friend who only hung around to buy pills.*

Dear Austin

You're alive.

I know because I'm Facebook friends with your mom.

I know because last night in a dream you stuck a butter knife to my throat.

I owe you money, big money, but I don't have that kind of cash.

What if I paid you back in facts?

Fact: you were my best friend before my drug dealer.

Ghost back with me to 2003, our lives the length of the Broad Street bridge to 7-Eleven. Red Bulls, RuneScape, Roughrider games. Easy, easy goodness.

What if, instead, I paid you with leftovers from my boyhood?

Take my club foot. Take the leech fastened to my thigh.

I want to owe you nothing, Austin. Not even a goodbye.

Here, take my sobriety. Crush it up. Smoke it. It's yours.

Dear Derek

I thought I saw you—dark and glowing under the sun, a fry
hanging from your mouth—but it was just another crow.

Daydreaming

Some of us have grandmas who drop
ice cubes in our soup. Some of us live
with burned tongues. I'm protected

in the kitchen but battered in the other
rooms of this world. There's another way
and I'm sure of it. Squint then squint

again. There—a chocolate chip cookie
recipe in the comment section instead
of eugenics. And there—a placemat

on the sidewalk that catches everything
my mouth fails to hold. Let me be a man
who cools that which is too hot to slurp,

a dishrag hung on my shoulder. Let me eat
in public with the birds and the babies
and those who shamelessly fill their faces.

Comment section II

countless lives

will be successful

A good friend
is a

junkie

A Junkie would willingly use

A band-aid over a

bleeding heart

What about

free   drugs for everyone

                    free   free
            free
free

Marriage

for Harper

In front of Shoppers, a man warms himself
with fentanyl. A stranger sheltering
from Vancouver's sting should not
shock me but always does. Do I offer
change, ask for a hoot?

Inside Shoppers, we shop for an easy meal,
antihistamines, Q-tips destined for ear
canals. You remind me to buy what I'd forget,
like the special floss that infiltrates my retainer.
My teeth, once rotting, unflossed, and unbrushed
for years, now have you on their team.

On the drive home, I recite my scheduled
breakdown. *We can't afford rent. Floss equals
more debt. The world is a wasteland.*

On the couch, a woman warms
a man with her body, sheltering
him from the sting.

Social media

Strangers want me dead,
but I am here, needle in arm,
veins blooming with 1,000 lilies.
The flowers, of course, are fragile.
Pull the needle out and this room will flutter
with petals that no invisible hand can arrange,

once more, into flowers.

They want me dead. Not the way my mom thought I was dead
but prayed for resurrection over cabernet, takeout, and CTV News.
They want me dead, dead. Dead like dinosaurs. Semen in the sewer dead.
But I am here, frying perogies for Grandma because she says I fry them best.

Notes

"Sweet soil" is a response to a Facebook comment published on a CBC Vancouver story titled "Why fentanyl is so deadly" on September 17, 2016.

"The cost of junk" is a response to a Facebook comment published on a CTV Vancouver story titled "Percentage of fatal ODs tied to fentanyl up 150% from last year: report" on November 10, 2017.

"Dog backwards is god" is a response to a Facebook comment published on a CBC Vancouver story titled "Why fentanyl is so deadly" on September 17, 2016.

"Policy proposal" is a response to a Facebook comment from a Medicine Hat court sheriff, in reference to Medicine Hat residents who inject drugs. The court sheriff published the comment in the "Official Medicine Hat Neighbourhood Watch" Facebook group in August 2019.

"Small deaths" is a response to a Facebook comment posted on a CTV Vancouver article titled "2020 is likely to be B.C.'s deadliest year for toxic drug overdoses" from December 27, 2020.

The process for the "body," "family," and "addicts" sections of "We met on 5th" is as follows: I searched "fentanyl addiction" in Google News and copy and pasted the contents of the first 20 news stories into a Word document. I used "control+f" to search "body," "family," and "addicts" within the resulting 41 pages of text (15,582 total words). I removed each sentence (and sometimes fragments of the previous and following sentences) containing each word to put in a new Word document. I joined words, sentence fragments, and complete sentences while also removing words and parts of words to craft the sections. No additional words were added. ("Body" appeared 12 times, "family" appeared 18 times, and "addicts" appeared 9 times.)

The comments that appear under "Dear Sam" and "Dear Mac Miller" were found on Facebook. For "Dear Sam," I searched CBC

Vancouver's Facebook page for posts containing "fentanyl" then selected comments from those posts to include. For "Dear Mac Miller," I searched CTV Vancouver's Facebook page for posts containing "naloxone" then selected comments from those posts to include.

"Comment section II" is an erasure of every Facebook comment posted to a CBC Vancouver article titled "B.C. moves to 'safe supply' as overdose deaths spike during COVID-19 pandemic" published on May 12, 2020.

Acknowledgements

Previous versions of poems from this book have appeared in *The Malahat Review, Contemporary Verse 2, Prairie Fire, subTerrain, Poetry Is Dead, Vallum, SAD Mag, The Quilliad, antilang.,* and the anthology *Plume Poetry 9.* Thank you to the editors of each.

Thank you to Shane Neilson, Jeremy Luke Hill, and the entire team at Gordon Hill Press for believing in this book and making it happen.

Thank you to Syd Danger for making my cover dreams come true.

I'm grateful to the Social Sciences and Humanities Research Council for its financial support.

Thank you to my poetry teachers and mentors: Sonnet L'Abbé, Jay Ruzesky, Robert Hilles, Susan Musgrave, and Sarah Yi-Mei Tsiang.

Thank you to my peers in the creative writing programs at Vancouver Island University and the University of British Columbia.

Thank you to my thesis advisor, Bronwen Tate, for showing me what this collection is truly about. Your guidance was invaluable.

I'm grateful for the barred owls at Morrell Nature Sanctuary. I wish you all the squirrels in the world.

My friends from the hospital, detox, treatment, sober living, and peer support—I am here today here because of you.

Many thanks to those who administer naloxone, distribute needles and pipes, and eat with whoever sits down at the table.

Thank you, Grandma, for your meals and stories, especially during my darkest days.

Thank you, Grandpa and Grandma, for your love and support.

Thank you, Mom and Dad, for everything you've given and sacrificed.

Charity, Angie, Dylan, Turner, and Logan—you've helped make me who I am.

I'm grateful for Maeve, my snuggly cat who might love food more than me.

And thank you, Harper, for accepting every version of me, for standing by my side in ways I couldn't have imagined, and for baking the best focaccia.

About the Author

Spenser Smith is a Regina-born poet, essayist, and photographer who recently moved to Winnipeg after ten years in B.C. His writing appears in *The Malahat Review, Prairie Fire, Contemporary Verse 2, The Capilano Review, Poetry Is Dead, Vallum, subTerrain, The Ex-Puritan*, and *SAD Mag*. In 2017, he was the poetry winner of the Blodwyn Memorial Prize. In 2020, he won an honourable mention in the Lush Triumphant Literary Awards. He holds a BA in creative writing and journalism from Vancouver Island University and an MFA in creative writing from the University of British Columbia.